Life's Constant Struggles to Success

By

Wilbert Skipper Jr.

Copyright © 2014
Authored by: Wilbert Skipper Jr.
All rights reserved.

ISBN: 1494982781

Contents

Acknowledgments

Introduction

Chapter   1   Family

Chapter   2   Believing in God

Chapter   3   True Friends

Chapter   4   Self-Pressure

Chapter   5   Believing in Yourself

Chapter   6   Coworkers

Chapter   7   Beware of the Dream Stealers

Special Thank You Section

Acknowledgments

I would like to thank my lovely wife, Sharon P. Skipper, for believing in this longtime dream of mine. I could not have done this without her support. I would also like to thank my late parents, Wilbert and Genevieve Skipper, for passing on all of their many teachings and unconditional love regarding my pursuit of success, as well as for instilling within me the morals, compassion, work ethic, respect, understanding, and ability to reach higher for my goals and dreams. Despite the fact that my father only achieved a ninth-grade education, he was able to retire from the federal government and operate a successful business as owner of Skipper's Hauling Service and Skipper's Inn restaurant in Seat Pleasant, Maryland. Neither of my parents believed in allowing someone to steal their dreams.

My lovely wife and me

My parents enjoying a few steps   My dear aunt Joyce

A special thanks to my late aunt Joyce Powell for all of her old-school talks incorporated with lots of wisdom, and for caring for my father while he was ill.

James Coach (Chip) was my best friend during most of my childhood years in southeast DC. His relentless work ethic, positive attitude, and true friendship were a valuable asset to my future development as a basketball player. We made each other better at our strengths and helped each other to become better people. His mother's disciplinary tactics and loving household were an extension of my own home.

Carlton Jackson was a fierce competitor, and he pushed my best friend, Chip, and me to be the best basketball players possible. He always had a positive outlook on our future success.

During my high school and college career, the late Stephen Boyd (Boo) was a true friend and loyal supporter. He always gave me constructive advice and encouragement toward my goals and dreams. He played a pivotal role as a true friend in my life.

I would like to thank Glenn Harris, Channel 8 WJLA sports talk host, for being a fatherly figure and a great role model for me during my teenage years, when I was growing up in southeast Washington, DC. Glenn Harris, by far, was the most positive influence at that time.

During my eighth- and ninth-grade years at Douglas Junior High School, Glenn Harris was a Great Leader. He always gave me tough encouragement. In addition to having a good, loving father, Glenn Harris also presented me with fatherly love, which helped me stay focused and determined to succeed. All of Glenn's advice paid off when I made the Douglas Junior High School basketball team as a ninth grader and became an all-star for our team. Being a Douglass Hawk was a big honor.

I would like to thank Sonia Grimes and family for their genuine support throughout my high school basketball career.

Ted Weeks of Champs Barbershop, thanks for your God-given barber skills, upon which I have relied on for many years and for your continuous support for my book project.

I would like to give thanks to Reverend Gault of Rolling Crest Worship Center for being an inspiration in my life. His divine knowledge and teaching of God's word has helped me strengthen my personal relationship with God.

I would like to thank John K Jenkins Sr., Pastor of First Baptist Church of Glenarden for his infinite godly insights and teaching about everyday living in the eyes of the Lord. This godly experience has been invaluable regarding my continuing spiritual growth.

I would like to thank Malick Wade and his team at Metro Area Consulting, LLC, for the design and management of my Kickstarter Campaign.

I would like to thank Fred Shepard Jr., Owner of F&S Photography, Images of Life, for his beautiful photography.

I would like to thank Darren Heath for his genuine support and friendship for over twenty-five years.

I would also like to thank Myron Thomas, business owner in southeast Washington, DC, for being a genuine supporter of my book project. He has truly been a blessing from God.

Thank you to Roland Grimes for giving me the opportunity to be a co-host of his Internet TV show, *"The Roland Grimes Show."* This experience was very beneficial for my growth.

Left to right: Eugene Hellams Jr., Roland Grimes, and Wilbert Skipper

I would like to thank Dr. Marcus S. Tappan and Associates, PC, of Silver Spring, Maryland, and his staff for their support in helping me to overcome my fear and anxiety of going to the dentist on a regular basis. This was a major milestone for me because I had not visited a dentist practice for more than ten years due to my fear. Now I have a smile that I am very proud to display!

Finally, I would like to thank all the backers, Emery Simmons and Anacostia High School Alumni who supported my kickstarter book campaign. We could not have done it without you!

Life's Constant Struggles to Success

Introduction

Often, success will not manifest until we first overcome obstacles and negativity. Most of the time, negative influences and surroundings can disrupt our paths to successfully achieving our goals. When we allow ourselves to digest and retain negative information, the road to success can become extremely difficult.

Unfortunately, in many cases people do not celebrate our successes until we become successful on a large scale. Therefore, we must have a great deal of self-determination, internal motivation, direction, and focus to sustain ourselves.

The road that we must travel to become successful in life is full of pitfalls. Sometimes these pitfalls can be so traumatic and difficult that we find ourselves doubting our own abilities to succeed. I truly believe that there are many people, including family members, who purposely try to block our paths to success.

It is very easy to say "no thanks" to the hard road that we must travel in order to become successful in life. Over 70 percent of the people I knew in my teenage years took a liking to negativity. They could not escape from the peer pressure of the "in-crowd," which kept them from working hard to achieve their goals and dreams. This behavior became a normal way of living for them.

Accepting disbelief and negative feelings directed at you in order to keep you from successfully achieving your goals can act like a cancer, which can spread throughout your body. After the disease (negativity) conquers your mind, there may be nothing left to do but to die. When you allow someone to destroy your motivation, sense of direction, and internal drive to succeed, you have killed your dreams.

I was determined to use the many negative influences I experienced in a positive way. I became so good at using this self-taught method that most people with whom I communicated, despite their negative way of thinking, became more open to a positive change in their own lives. I truly believe that the desire and hunger for success can be a life-long experience, which can help many people in your circles. The more we learn how to turn a negative situation into a positive one, the better the outcome will be.

Sometimes while you are traveling that road to success, you must exhale the negative energy and inhale the positive energy. I believe that once you build up enough endurance and positive energy, your physical vibes will help minimize the negative energy that you receive from other people.

Being able to master the "I can-make it" belief, despite being told that you cannot, can be extremely critical in determining your level of success. Always remember that the race to success in life is not a sprint; instead, it is a marathon.

Life's constant struggles can be a journey of gratification as long as you are willing to pursue these struggles with an intense internal and external work ethic. Stay positive, think positively, walk positively, and stay focused while working toward your goals and dreams.

Chapter 1

Family

When we think of family, we generally think of any group of persons closely related by blood—parents, children, uncles, aunts, and cousins. There is an old proverb, "Blood is thicker than water," but what most of us realize is that our families can also be our worst enemies. No one, including family, is exempt from being negative and disruptive to your path to success. While this may not be true for every family, I believe it is more of a rule than an exception.

Some family members do not aid you in your struggles to succeed until they believe that you are going to achieve your goals. Also, how about those family members who want to acknowledge your success only *after* your struggles are over?

As a ten-year-old boy, I can remember very clearly how some of my family members told me that I would never amount to anything. Quite naturally, I was slightly confused, but I quickly told myself that my motivation, sense of direction, and internal drive to succeed would prove them wrong.

Despite their feelings, I continued to keep a positive attitude towards my dreams and goals.

Although it is discouraging when a family member chooses not to support your individual efforts to succeed, it can be very beneficial if you learn how to turn negative energy into a positive force for drive and determination. Despite the love that blood family should have for each other, we often find that unconditional love fails when negativity has infested one's train of thought. This truly suggests that jealousy, envy, and hatred can poisoned the positive feelings one should associate with family.

It is difficult to succeed while being negatively influenced by someone who does not want to see you achieve; however, you can listen without letting that poison kill your spirit. Remember that when a person is always negative, he or she is displaying a sign of personal unhappiness, and that sometimes people channel this lack of confidence in themselves into being negative toward or unsupportive of you.

I have developed ten family commandments, which all families should teach their children.

1) Thou shalt love family always in an unconditional way.
2) Thou shalt not discriminate against family wishes, despite personal feelings.
3) Thou shalt support family based on what is best through the grace of God.
4) Thou shalt encourage family to be the best that they can be—always.

5) Thou shalt not mistake hate for love with family.

6) Thou shalt assist family when they need help as they travel the hard road to success.

7) Thou shalt pray for thy family.

8) Thou shalt encourage children to respect and support the ten family commandments.

9) Thou shalt always put God first while supporting family.

10) Thou shalt show gratification and love toward the successes of other family members.

The quality of the relationship you have with a family member will ultimately determine how much love and support he or she gives you while you are trying to become successful in life.

In 2001, I developed the theory of *solid relationship laws*, which is very important in the family structure and in individual relationships.

God—Have a spiritual relationship with the Lord that begins with putting God first in your life.

Trust—Believe in your family or mate in an honest and trusting way.

Honesty—Do not cheat or lie; be upright, sincere, genuine, and always open to dialogue.

Communication—Be open to talk about anything in life, and communicate honestly with each other.

Compromise—Settle differences with a compromise, and be willing to meet the other halfway.

Life can be a struggle for us all, but we must believe in God and ourselves despite what some family members may negatively think about our future prosperity and success. We must stay motivated and focus on achieving our goals and dreams. Do not be afraid to travel in the waters of success without family support.

Chapter 2

Believing in God

Believing in God begins with putting God first, understanding that he rules the universe and life within it, and welcoming his spirit to develop a personal relationship with him.

Developing a personal relationship with God requires a commitment that will allow you to be open to his presence always. You will find yourself turned off by ungodly things that can steer you in the wrong direction. You must build your inner and outer self to be one as you make your relationship with God more solid. Building your inner self consists of having strong faith and belief. Building your outer self consists of ensuring you resist the worldly distractions that exist in our daily lives. Having a relationship with God will allow you to maintain a clear mind when things in your life are not going well. The unconditional love and joy that comes from having a relationship with God will change your life. Anyone with an open heart and willingness to accept God can begin to experience this great feeling.

Knowing and believing does not compare to anything that exists on this earth. When worldly issues take place, sometimes we forget that God is the almighty giant who cannot only move mountains, but more importantly, can also permanently re-create our total well-being. Sometimes we do not receive the full understanding of God's work until we find ourselves in trouble or in an unfortunate situation. One should have his or her own belief in God's powers before encountering a negative person or trying situation. I have believed in this principle for most of my life.

I can remember quite vividly, while growing up in the Catholic Church, saying to myself that despite the many denominations that existed, there is only one God. As a young kid, I continued to pray to god on a daily basis with the understanding that he would always be with me.

Being able to get high on God's spiritual powers is the ultimate feeling. Being able to feel God's motion of movement within your physical body allows a connection with your mental state of being, which can empower you to greatness. Being able to witness God's work through your own belief is physically, emotionally, spiritually, and mentally gratifying.

Although, I am not the most religious person in the world, my one-on-one spiritual relationship with God is at a very high level. I invite God to live within me and to touch my mind and spirit on a daily basis. To me, God is my judge, my insurer of success, authority maker, always-right spirit, feeling of joy and personal healing forever.

Everyone needs to develop his or her own private and sacred spiritual relationships with God. The almighty creator will not let you down, despite your mistakes. We must always remember that God is a forgiving God.

Loving God and knowing that he is an unlimited provider for all of our needs is truly a blessing.

I believe that the godly way to being is the true way to freedom within you. Believing in God is the best drug that we can digest.

Being able to build yourself through your belief in God is the best personal treasure that you can receive. Your belief in God should be unconditional and relished by your true, Godly beliefs.

Believing in God first and in yourself second is a good recipe for positive living. You should not look for a man or woman to validate your relationship with God. God's love is real, and he lives in us every day. He is the only one who can change your life. I will always give God praise. Open your mind and hearts to God's forever blessings of commitment, spiritual guidance, and love for all people. When you commit to your belief in God, the world you once knew will suddenly change.

Praying is a very important part of building your relationship with God. When I pray to God for my future success, there is a tune of happiness that I can hear ringing in my ear. The song is titled, "I believe in my relationship with God." When you open your mind to God's work, unbelievable experiences begin to manifest.

To know God is to love God unconditionally and to experience his divine work of power, which no man can match. People, who think with a demonic mind, may test your belief in God. You must be able to defuse their negative energy by allowing God's work to destroy the moment of disparity. Having experienced this myself through prayer, I can say that it is like having the Holy Ghost enter your body and take control of your speaking; you will be empowered by this real miracle moment. When you hit a brick wall in life with no out-plan in place, you could very easily give up and accept your circumstances. But to say no to the obstacles in your path and fight the battle with God leading the way is the most awesome experience in which one can participate.

When you hear people say that there is no God, you can only imagine how terrible it is not to have a personal relationship with him. Without him, nothing is possible. Before my mother passed away in 1982, she told me never to question God's work. I refuse to submit to the devil's demonic spirit force. When you allow God to work through you and to provide a wall of protection and covering, the demonic spirits will be heard but not accepted.

These experiences will truly become a godly touchdown for you. When you score through God's work, your opponent does not matter. You will always win the game. I personally know that God wants me to be at peace with myself so that I can receive his blessings while reaching back to help others. I truly understand what God wants me to do, and I am in line to do just that. My passion for being positive and empowering people through action and effective communication is my calling from God. I want and will become the best person I can be while committing to this journey.

I can only hope and pray that all people, at some point in their lives, will come to know God and develop a one-on-one spiritual relationship with him.

One of the best godly decisions that I made after playing basketball at Anacostia High School was to accept a basketball scholarship to attend Southeast Community Junior College in Fairbury, Nebraska. This decision would change my life forever.

My prayers and faith in God gave me the strength that I needed mentally and physically to overcome any obstacles that came my way throughout this journey.

In 1978, upon my arrival to the Southeast Community College Campus, which was nearly 2,100 miles away from home, I quickly learned that I was one of only eleven blacks in a small town of about 5,100 people. This was a cultural shock to me. This was also a real challenge, but I was determined to use this experience to build on my faith and belief in myself in becoming the best student and athlete at SCC.

I decided to be a volunteer at Fairbury High School for the youth organization. This experience allowed me the opportunity to become more comfortable within the community.

I took this opportunity to better my grades and basketball talents so that after graduating from SCC, I could play basketball at a Division I basketball school. Thanks to the support of Fluff Parker and the late Harold Bates (Executive III basketball coaches). They believed in me and gave me the opportunity to play on the youth basketball team. With their contacts and relationships with SCC basketball staff, I had the opportunity to get a basketball scholarship.

Through hard work and dedication, I was able to become a very successful junior college basketball player. I also had the opportunity to meet with Nebraska Congressman Charles Thone. This meeting took place at the US Capitol in 1978. He welcomed me on becoming a student Athlete at SCC.

Meeting with Congressman Thone at the Capitol

Believing in myself allowed me the opportunity to further my education at George Washington University (GWU) in Washington, DC, on a basketball scholarship after my career at Southeast Community College in

1980. If I did not believe in my own ability to succeed, I might have killed my own dreams. After graduating from SCC, many naysayers said that I could not succeed in pursuing my dreams of becoming a successful basketball player on a Division I level. Many people believe in themselves, but they still need someone to validate them. This is a sign of lack of confidence and belief in your abilities to succeed and fulfill your dreams. I was determined not to let this happen to me. I had to overcome a seriously injury while playing at GWU. I separated my right shoulder while attempting to block a shot. I was not able to play for seven games. I later had to have surgery and through God's healing, daily prayer and meditation, I was able to come back stronger.

I constantly remind my daughters—Yasmine, Bria, and stepdaughter, Ebony—about the importance of believing in God and yourself, despite what others may think of you. Unfortunately, the world in which we live today is infested with negativity and dream stealers. If you are weak minded and unsure of yourself, you might become their next victim.

Always remember that the almighty God is watching over you and that during times of hardship and despair, you can count on him. Keep God in your life throughout your travels to success. You can make it with God leading the way. You must constantly say, "Yes, I can…yes, I can," and believe in your heart that God is the almighty power of authority who will forever oversee your life. If you believe in God and walk with God's claimed favor for you, the door to *success* will be unlocked and waiting for you. Success with God is worth life's constant struggles to succeed. Let us meet one day in God's success line.

I can only thank the many people of Fairbury, Nebraska, for their warm support and help during my tenure at SCC. This experience prepared me for many future life experiences. I will always cherish the SCC family. Amen!

Chapter 3

True Friends

This chapter is dedicated to one of my best friends, the late Stephen Boyd (Boo). He set an example of what a true friend should be, and I will never forget the impact that he had on my life.

First row center: Carlton
Second row (left to right): Skipper, "Chip," and "Boo."

I believe that *true* friends are forever, but true friends are often very hard to find. How many times have we been hurt or betrayed by our so-called true friends?

How many times have we truly supported a friend's successes but did not get the same treatment in return? How many times have we asked God why our so-called friends did not support our positive efforts? How many times have we terminated a friendship because of distrust, lack of respect, or nonsupport? How many times have our so-called true friends purposely tried to distract us from our paths to success?

We could continue to look back over the times when we have been let down by our friends, but it is truly a blessing from God when we can make the best out of a negative situation with a friend. I can remember talking to a so-called true friend about my business goals in life. I could see his negative facial expressions, and I immediately tuned him out, knowing that he would not be supportive. His actions were a blessing because it gave me the will power to distract and dismiss his negative thoughts and continue to pursue my dreams.

Sometimes we have to shield ourselves from the "want-to-be-friends" because, in most cases, they have one thing in mind: to destroy you and your dreams.

True friends are supposed to be an extension of your blood family, providing you with unconditional love and support for your struggles in life. Having a true friend with unconditional feelings of love for you is just like having money in the bank. You know that they will be there for you no matter what. My mother used to tell me that when you die, you are very lucky if you have one true friend shed tears of sadness and joy. I guess in some cases, it is only natural for you to be naive or fooled by people whom you imagine to be your true friends. My mother also used to tell me that money, success, and the constant struggles in life would reveal the truth about people who consider themselves to be true friends. How can someone consider himself or herself to be a true friend when he or she does not know the meaning of the word *loyalty*?

When I was fourteen years old, I spoke with an elderly man about life. One of the most important pieces of information he shared with me was that wisdom and knowledge come from good and bad experiences in life. He then went on to tell me that living your life does not have to be a bad thing, and that there is something good in everything that is bad.

After thinking very hard about this elderly man's theory on living life, I began to stop judging a book by its cover; instead, I began looking at the contents of the book. Do not cling to the hype from so-called friends; instead, cherish the unconditional loving support and comfort that only a true friend can provide. Being able to surround yourself with a positive shield will help you stay focused while traveling the road to success.

I would like to thank the following true friends: the late Stephen Boyd (Boo), Jon Jones, James Coach (Chip), Lorenzo Cain, Ted Weeks, Malick Wade, Roland Grimes, William Jones (Koonie), Cornell Smith, Fred

Shepard Jr., the late Harlan G. Hopkins, Stacy Robinson, Darren Heath, Terence Hawkins, Penny Elliott, Reginald Williams (Big Wheel), the late Keith Mayo, Carlton Jackson, Sheldon Edwards, Eugene Thompson, John Williams, and Mike Brey (head basketball coach for Notre Dame University). I thank these people for being true friends and positive supporters of my goals and dreams.

Penny Elliott

During my student athletic career at George Washington University, my best friend on campus was Penny Elliott, a six-foot, ten-inch forward/center for our basketball team. There were many days and nights when we would talk about our goals outside of basketball. His friendship and support were unconditional. Life does not say that everyone you meet will become a true friend, but I do believe that a true friendship will reveal itself in ways that you will recognize and value.

Mike Brey was my roommate and a true friend in every sense of the word. Mike and I often talked about how we wanted to be a role model to young men. He often talked about the importance of being the best person that you could be every day. He was very inspiring, motivating, and a positive person. Mike and I were the starting guards and tri-captains on the 1981–82 GWU basketball team. His personality, people skills, and hard work allowed him to become a very successful college basketball coach at Duke, Delaware, and currently at Notre Dame University.

From left to right: Mike Brey, Paul Gracza, and me

Below are some characteristics of a true friend, who…

- listens to your troubles or concerns with an open and objective frame of mind
- supports your goals in a positive way
- tells you the truth regardless of whether it may hurt you

- disagrees with you because it is the right thing to do instead of agreeing with you just to keep the friendship
- prays for you throughout your journey in life
- refrains from being a dream stealer

True friendship of any kind is a valuable asset to rely upon. A true friend does not come into your life with negative feelings toward you or your goals. A true friend is like a breath of fresh air: "It feels very good." I do not know how many true friends will cross your path in life, but I believe that you will not have to second-guess yourself when it happens!

When I was very young, I was fortunate enough to meet several of my true friends on the basketball court. We had a strong interest in basketball and had many of the same goals. Our dreams were to play in the NBA. Through trust and honesty, we later established a true friendship.

A true friend is a good thing, and most of all, it is truly a blessing from God.

Chapter 4

Self-Pressure

Even the word *"pressure"* can be intimidating to people. When we add the word *"self"* to pressure, we might begin to picture huge weights sitting on our shoulders, but self-pressure can be used in either a positive, not just a negative way.

Let me first talk about the negative aspects of self-pressures. When you are trying to succeed at achieving your goals, one of the most important elements is to stay positive; therefore, when you tell yourself that your goals are not achievable and are unrealistic within yourself, the words *"defeat* and *"failure"* become one of the weights that settle upon you. Being able to develop a shield against envy, negativity, jealousy, and failure will help you combat the struggles faced while traveling the road to success.

Sometimes, we may feel that when no one else believes in us, we should not believe in ourselves. Over the years, I have learned that refusing to receive a non-believer's responses about my individual goals is like saying no thanks to food that I do not like. It really is not that hard to do. Many people seek the advice of people who do not believe in them. By doing this, it makes it easier for you to doubt your own ability to succeed. Often times, people are afraid to stand alone and because of this fear, they fail.

Defeat and failure can also be used in a positive way. When we learn from our mistakes and continue to work hard at achieving our goals, we are turning a negative into a positive. I have never allowed myself to accept failure. My parents taught me how to defy failure and work hard for success at a very young age.

My parents taught me that dedication and hard work would pay off if you stay focused. They dedicated time and motivation to my siblings and me. My parents made sure that I stayed committed to homework and basketball practice. They were always there for me.

How do you head off failure? Try these five steps:

Step 1

Think positively at all times; always look for the good in something bad.

Step 2

Build an internal and external shield to combat negativity.

- Keep a positive mind-set.
- Stay focused.
- Do not accept negative energy from people.
- Walk with God's favor.
- Be confident in yourself.

Step 3

- Do not buy into the "misery loves company" theory under any circumstances.
- Stay away from people who envy your drive to succeed.

Step 4

- Learn how to motivate yourself with your dreams and goals.
- Be prepared to reinvent yourself, if necessary.

Step 5

- Do not look for someone to believe in your goals more than you do.
- Do not look for validation from others.

At one point, while a freshman basketball player at Southeast Community College, I phoned my parents in Seat Pleasant, Maryland, because I thought that my basketball coach was being unfair with me. He had decided to decrease my playing time so that another player who was not as productive could play more. I disagreed with his decision and mentioned it to the team. Because of my actions, he decided to discipline me. My mother told me that if I was unhappy, I could come home. My father, on the other hand, told me that I should not buck the system. He said that I should stay in school, improve my relationship with my coach, and focus on my basketball career after junior college.

First, what I learned from this experience was that making a rush decision about something often leads to a less-than-desirable outcome. I also learned to be more tactful and to think first before reacting to disappointment.

I went to practice the next day with a new attitude, and the turnaround for me was an awesome experience. After the next two games, I had regained the starting shooting guard position. I succeeded by putting pressure on myself to do what was best for my future.

At the end of my freshman year, I finished the year by making the Second Team All-Conference and All Region while averaging sixteen points per game.

At the start of my sophomore year, I was a pre-season All-American candidate. At the end of the year, I was the third leading scorer in four states (Iowa, Kansas, Missouri, and Nebraska) while averaging twenty-five points per game. I also became Southeast Community College's all time leading scorer in two years, with 1,226 points.

In addition to those achievements, I graduated in two years with an associate's degree in pre-business administration. I also made First Team All-Conference, All Region, and honorable mention All-American before signing a basketball scholarship to be a student athlete at George Washington University in Washington, DC.

There are many self-pressures and affirmations, which we can use every day to motivate ourselves and to help us achieve our goals. Below are just a few affirmations that you should include your daily life:

- Use your God-given talents to the fullest every day.
- Tell yourself every day that you are an achiever and a champion of yourself
- Remind yourself of how good it feels to be you.
- Do not take no for an answer.
- Do not let someone else kill or steal your dreams.
- Tell yourself that outside of God, you are in control of your dreams.
- Use negativity from others in a positive way.
- Tell yourself that staying motivated, being positive, and remaining focused are important keys to your success.
- Self-inflict the will to win every day.
- Incorporate God's validation of you in your daily life, and welcome his favor.

I was given an invitation to try out for the Washington, DC, youth game team. I shared this exciting moment with some of my friends and family while looking for their support. Unfortunately, many of them did not believe that I would make the team.

At the beginning of tryouts, there were at least 150 participants. After the final cut, I was left standing with eleven other basketball players who had made the team. Some of my teammates were Sidney Lowe, Former NC State Basketball Coach; Derrick Whittenburg, former University of Fordham Basketball Coach and 1982–83 NCAA Basketball Champions at North Carolina State; Percy White (DeMatha High School); Ezel Stuart (Wakefield High School in Virginia); Anthony Martin (Mackin High School); Curtis Campbell (Ballou High School); and Phil Ward (Coolidge High School).

Despite the disbelievers, I was one of twelve District of Columbia basketball players selected to represent the youth games in Fort Worth, Texas, and I was able to reach another goal in life. It was truly a great achievement for me.

Unfortunately, one day, despite my success as a basketball player, I mingled with the wrong crowd. Officer Sam, who policed our high school, helped me turn things around. He gave me a new outlook on life after I made a bad mistake that could have crippled my future basketball career.

One afternoon during regular school hours, I cut class with a group of classmates. We decided to smoke marijuana in the bathroom. After we finished smoking, a school officer, who had smelled the smoke in the hallway, approached us. We were thankful to get a second chance for this bad choice. Not everyone took advantage of this opportunity. However, after this incident was over, I made a sincere commitment to God and myself not to make this mistake again. I think that it is very important not to participate in wrongdoing to fit in with others.

Although I made those mistakes, I did learn from them and had the opportunity to attend five-star basketball camp. I was thrilled to for this opportunity. This experience allowed me to highlight my basketball talent against the nation's best players. The exposure that I received awarded me over one hundred basketball letters from colleges regarding my talent.

I was able to establish a good rapport with Howard Garfinkel (CEO, president) during my stay at this prestigious basketball camp. He taught me to be discipline, patience and most of all to think before I react.

After my junior year at GWU, I had the opportunity to go back to five-star basketball camp to work as a counselor. Five-star basketball camp is where high school basketball players participate with college coaches and counselors to improve their basketball skills and to become recognized. It was truly an honor to play competitively against Trent Tucker (retired New York Knicks), Vern Fleming (retired Indiana Pacers), and Perry Moss (retired Bullets and Boston Celtics)— all of whom played successfully in the NBA. I also had the opportunity to play against John Calipari

(University of Kentucky head basketball coach) and NCAA Champions in 2011.

Despite the fact that I did not fulfill my goal of becoming an NBA basketball player after my career at George Washington University, I was determined to continue improving myself. My NBA is now to motivate kids and adults and encourage young people to be positive, think positive, and do the right thing. It is important to remember that being unable to achieve a goal does not mean that you have failed! You will make mistakes along the way while pursuing your goals, but the experiences should make you a better person. Believe in God, believe in yourself, stay positive, and remain motivated and focused, which will all make your journey in life worthwhile.

During my four years of playing college basketball, I scored 1,912 points. I also made the Eastern Eight all rookie team and honorable mention All Big East in 1981. Currently, I am in the top ten field goal percentages for a guard at GWU. During the 1981–82 basketball season, my field goal percentage was 54.1 percent. This field goal percentage based on research from Pennington Greene (DC basketball blog) was one of the best individual yearly percentages for a guard in the nation professionally and in college. I had the opportunity to try out for the Philadelphia 76ers in 1982. In 1984, the Bay State Bombardiers of the Continental Basketball Association, CBA, drafted me in the first round.

I was determined to be the best basketball player that I could be. My work ethics, dedication, determination and focus allowed me to prevail.

Applying positive self-pressure is another way to motivate you in regards to your future goals. You should always shoot for the moon, and if you fall short, you will still be with the stars. Holding yourself accountable and responsible for doing the right thing in God's eyes is the way to *success* and *prosperity*, which you are worthy of having.

Grades as Important
As 'Hoops' at Anacostia

By Gary Davidson
Special to The Washington Post

Calvin Stith considers himself lucky. While most other District basketball coaches have only one season goal—the Interhigh league title—Stith has two goals he considers within reach.

Stith makes it very clear that the first priority for his team, which has won its first four games, is the Interhigh crown. But his second goal is one that could last his players a lifetime: a college education.

"I see their counselors and teachers as much as I see them," Stith said of his squad. "We never won a basketball title. That's my challenge. The other goal—for the kids to go away to school and get a (college) degree—is

The success of the Indians can be traced to patient, hard work by Stith, whose record after three years stood at only 25-37. But a 3-15 mark in 1975-76 grew to 11-11 last year, and now Stith has an experienced, all-senior starting five.

Three players have started for Stith since their sophomore year. Forward Wilbert Skipper, who at 6-5 is averaging 24.8 points per game, 6-foot-2½ James Coach, also a forward, who pulls down 15 rebounds and 12 points a game, and 6-foot guard Clarence Murdock. Dexter Price, a 6-1 guard who is second on the team in scoring at 18.3 points per contest, and 6-6 center Andre Adams are playing their second seasons on the starting squad.

Wilbert Skipper   **Randy Crawford**

SCC's Skipper Named All-Region

Wilbert Skipper, Southeast Community College - Fairbury freshman cager, has been named to the All-Region IX second team, according to an announcement made this week by Steve Hunter, SCC coach.

Skipper, son of Mr. and Mrs. Wilbert Skipper of Washington, D.C., boasted a 15-5 per game scoring average during the Bombers' 17-11 season, as he hit 50 percent of his field goal attempts (186-371) and 75 percent of his charity tosses (63-84).

Jones totaled 450 points for the season, a 16 points per game average. He shot 51 percent from the field and 62 percent at the charity stripe.

Jones and Crawford were among the Bomber rebounding leaders, pulling down 232 and 215 caroms respectively.

Joining Skipper and Crawford on the second team are Dick Noll of York College, Dan Lucht of Northeast-Norfolk, and Terry Tripplett of Nebraska Western-Scottsbluff.

W-H All-Junior College

First Team

Player, School (Votes)	Ht.	Year	Avg.
Kevin McNamara, Neb. Western (15)	5-11	So.	16.0
Kevin Bromley, Mid-Plains (12)	6-2	Fr.	18.8
Kevin Patterson, Mid-Plains (13)	6-7	So.	18.8
Dick Uhing, NE of Norfolk (15)	6-3	So.	21.8
Terry Holbert, York (10)	6-6	Fr.	18.6

Second Team

Wilbert Skipper, SE of Fairbury (7)	6-3	Fr.	16.0
Dick Noll, YORK (5)	6-0	So.	12.5
Dan Lucht, NE of Norfolk (6)	6-7	Soph.	12.5
Terry Triplett, Neb. Western (9)	6-7	So.	15.0
Randy Crawford, SE of Fairbury (7)	6-5	Fr.	20.4

Honorable (9 or more votes) — Steve Garretson, McCook,

Hunter Guardedly Optimistic About Southeast Cage Squad

Guarded optimism.

That's how Steve Hunter, men's basketball coach at Southeast Community College - Fairbury described his view of his 1979-80 Bomber squad.

"We have the potential to be a very good team," he said, "but with our schedule, we'll have to see a good team effort in every game if we are to be successful."

Local cage fans will have the opportunity to get a look at the Bombers in action Tuesday, Nov. 6, when the Southeast squad hosts its pre-season preview.

Scheduled for 7:30 p.m., the preview scrimmage will feature the potential Bomber starters against other team members during the first half. Hunter said he will probably do considerable switching of players in the second half of action.

Special highlights of Tuesday's pre-season preview will be a slam dunk contest and a Bomber Cage Club drawing.

Some Familiar Faces

What can Bomber fans expect to see in Tuesday's scrimmage? Among other things, there ... be some familiar faces.

Hunter said he is counting on McKinney and Skipper to be the team leaders.

"They know the system, they've been through one year, and most importantly, they know the level of competition we face," Hunter said. "And ... ... it's hard to tell the ...

He plans to put those strengths to good use, as the Bombers will be fast breaking as much as possible.

"We won't be able to slow down, since many of the teams we'll face will be bigger and stronger," he said.

Though he plans to let his ...

... said, "so I'm looki... improvement from ... that area of our ga...

Because of the ... offense and the f... fense, Hunter and ... use a number of p... won't be seeing fo... players a game." ... think we're lookin... nine or more, depe... game."

Open Season

The Bombers op... Wednesday, Nov. ... Cowley County C... Kansas City, Kan... play in the classic... return home Nov ... tain Highland Co... lege.

And this year, ... will face the Uni... braska - Lincoln ... in a Thursday, De...

Hunter said th... goal of winning ... Community Col... Conference title ... that, we'll just ... into place.

"If we can end ... tourney with at le... be happy with th... said.

Mike McKinney   (Wilbert Skipper)

W-H All-Junior College

First Team

Player, School	Ht.	Year	Avg.
Kevin Bromley, Mid-Plains	6-2	Soph	17.8
Jim Donnelly, Neb. Western	6-1	Soph	12.7
Darrel Reshaw, McCook	6-5	Fr.	16.6
Wilbert Skipper, SE-Fairbury	6-5	Soph	24.9
Darryl Williams, Neb. Western	6-4	Soph	19.4

Second Team

Player, School	Ht.	Year	Avg.
Les Adelung, Mid-Plains	6-0	Soph	18.3
Todd Sohl, NTCC of Norfolk	6-1	Soph	18.8
Mike McKinney, SE-Fairbury	6-7	Soph	11.9
Steve Garretson, McCook	6-2	Soph	13.7
Steve Wisdom, York	6-5	Soph	19.3

Honorable mention — Jerry Shinn, McCook. Howard Dordlinger, Central Tech. Gary Monroe, Nebraska Western. Al Johnson, Platte. Stan Hearns, Southeast-Fairbury. Dana Childs and Dale Blum, NTCC of Norfolk. Danny Lewis, York.

(Top Region Scorers) in four States Wyoming

Sophomore year   Iowa   Nebraska

SCC Tied   Kansas

Individual Scoring

Player	School	GP	FG	FT	TP	AVG
L. Griffin	Sheridan	28	214	207	735	26.3
Kevin Jones	LCCC	28	270	186	726	26.
W. Skipper	S.E. Fairbury	27	282	113	673	25.1
Tony Nardin	Casper	27	230	143	619	22.9
Rick Garrison	Sheridan	29	214	162	650	22.4
B. Deboer	Powell	28	247	117	609	21.7
D. Williams	Neb. Western	30	237	106	580	19.5
Smith	Central Wyo	25	189	104	482	19.3
S. Wisdom	York	24	183	98	454	19.3
Les Adelung	Mid-Plains	...	...	...	...	...

43

1978–79 Southeast Community College basketball team

1979–80 Southeast Community College basketball team

1979–80 First team W-H All region and all conference players

44

Chapter 5

Believing in Yourself

According to Webster's Dictionary, the definition of *"believe"* is to have a firm conviction as to the reality or goodness of something and to accept trustfully and on faith in the natural goodness of man." The definition of *"yourself"* is "that identical one that is you, your normal health, or same condition, "oneself."

Believing in yourself simply means trusting in your own ability to succeed, no matter what you set out to accomplish and despite the negativity that you may encounter. Do not believe those who, out of spite, want to see you fail.

I have always believed in my parents, my true friends, and the role models who contributed to my individual successes in life. Sometimes we believe that we can do everything for ourselves, but I disagree. Having good people in your life is worth living for!

Growing up in southeast Washington, DC, was not only a challenge in my life, but also a meaningful and life changing experience that I would not trade for anything. Sometimes my surroundings were filled with gunfire, drugs, erratic behavior, and instability, but my belief in God, family morals, and discipline kept me out of harm's way. I can remember sitting on my bed asking God to please allow my family to one day be able to move to a better area.

My basketball was my best friend, my girlfriend, and my source of comfort. I really felt that one day my basketball success would allow me to revisit my old neighborhood and inspire other kids with my story. I am sure that there are still many kids living in the Washington metropolitan area who have stories similar to mine. I truly believe that in everything bad that happens, there is a positive message from which one can learn and benefit. Negative experiences can transform into a positive outlook on life.

My mother used to say to my brothers and sisters that if they could not say anything good about someone, then they should not say anything at all. I was able to use my mother's theory and incorporate it into my everyday walk in life. Despite the good people who were in my life, I can remember clearly how many people in my neighborhood would tell me that I should give up on my dreams and just accept living without a purpose. Because my neighborhood was tough, most kids did not have any direction and were limited to their surroundings. Some of the kids did not have role models in their lives and were from a broken family, or their parents were on drugs and were not instrumental in their lives. Most kids were just trying to survive. I realized then that one of my goals was to one-day reach back to help those who were just like me.

There were many nights when my so-called friends and teenage girls would laugh at me because I chose to play basketball over going to the movies and to parties. While my friends were partying and having fun, I was dribbling my basketball and shooting one hundred jump shots in the dark. This work ethic helped me to improve my basketball shooting accuracy.

If you can make it in southeast Washington, DC, or any environment where drugs, violence, erratic behavior, and instability are prevalent, then you can make it anywhere.

When I was between the ages of nine and eleven, I used to go door-to-door in my apartment complex (Wellington Park in southeast Washington) to take out my neighbors' trash for a quarter. With the money I earned, I bought my first pair of Chuck Taylor All Star tennis shoes. It was very important for me to establish my independence at an early age. Many kids in my neighborhood were too proud to take out someone's trash.

At the same time, some of my friends used to laugh at me and tell me that I was wasting my time by playing basketball. My belief in myself allowed me to become very comfortable with being alone with my basketball. I learned that sometimes you have to separate yourself from family and friends while you work to pursue your dreams.

Our apartment complex was approximately two blocks from the projects—half a mile from Barry Farms and the Park Chester Community, which were very tough neighborhoods. I played some of my best basketball pickup games in those neighborhoods. Being able to survive and prosper while living in Wellington Park apartments allowed me to build internal and external strength, which helped me weather many storms.

It is easy to dwell on the negative rather than the positive. To help battle this, my mother made sure that I understood the importance of doing daily self-reflection. You learn more about yourself when you are willing to look within yourself, which helps build character. Also, meditating gives you a completely new perspective on yourself and your journey in life.

I can vividly remember a time during my sophomore year in junior college when I was doing some heavy soul searching to find out more about myself. I realized that life is full of good and bad experiences. As long as you learn from them, you will be able to see the light at the end of the tunnel. Believing in yourself is an awesome natural high. Self-confidence can be a powerful motivational tool. When this is present, alive, and working, the obstacles and struggles in your life become secondary.

My late father explained to me how you could educate yourself without attending college. With his advice, I developed a three-step discipline that consisted of reading the dictionary, thesaurus and listening to older people. These old schools ways of learning allowed me at a young age to jump-start the process of higher learning. I learned how to spell different words and use them correctly. This method taught me how to be discipline. Shortly after being consistent with this practice, I saw positive changes in me—in my vocabulary, articulation, and way of thinking. I also became highly motivated to speak about life as a whole; I believe that everyone is born with a God-given talent, which can be enhanced by believing in yourself, and I desired to share that knowledge.

Investing in yourself is one of the most important investments you can make toward your future. There are two positive words that begin with the letter *"F,"* which you should store in your mind:

Fortitude—The ability to withstand difficulties, fear, uncertainty, and risk.

Faith—Belief and trust in and loyalty to God; complete trust; something that is believed with strong conviction.

There are two negative words that begin with the letter *"F"* that you should dismiss from your mind:

Failure—Omission of occurrence or performance; lack of success; a state of inability to perform.

Fear—To be afraid of, consider with, or expect with alarm; to feel fear in oneself; to be afraid or apprehensive.

In late 2008, I established Reaching Back, a program designed to help young people understand the importance of hard work, staying positive, and remaining focused on their goals.

The two goals below are as follows:

Reaching—Extending your internal and external reach to help people of all cultures and walks of life who are open to life's many teachings.

Back—Being able to look back at all the good and bad that played a vital role in your life. Being able to share your experiences with others.

I believe that these two goals will help to empower and motivate our youth in their movement toward a positive outcome in life.

Self-Help Tools

- Develop a one-on-one relationship with God that will help build your belief and faith.
- You must stay focused and concentrate on what is most important for you to do in order to achieve your goals in life.
  - Education
  - Work ethic
  - Attitude
  - Confidence in yourself
- Surround yourself with positive-thinking people who believe in you, support you, and who will give you constructive criticism when needed.
- Set forth realistic goals for yourself. Do not put yourself in a position to fail.

- Know when it is your opportunity to shine. Do not be afraid to seize the moment.
- Walk through your dreams with a visual picture of yourself and your goals. See yourself as being successful.

I once saw Stacey Robinson (Dunbar High School and Washington, DC, basketball legend) at our George Washington University vs. Virginia University Basketball game at the Smith Center. During the first half of the game, our team was overpowered by the presence of first team All-American and future NBA lottery pick Ralph Sampson. Stacy Robinson caught my attention before the start of the second half and encouraged me to shoot the basketball. By receiving this positive encouragement from a true friend, and believing that I could play better, I went on to score twenty-three points in the second half.

Learning how to deal with negative situations in life, while maintaining balance and focus, is a very important part of achieving your goals. Having a strong will, along with seeking God and his guidance will allow you to minimize outside distractions. You cannot give up on your dreams just because one door closes. You must use your desire to achieve and your desire to rise above negativity as constant motivational tools.

Believing in yourself is very important in the pursuit of your dreams and goals. Despite the challenges and obstacles that you may face in your life, with God leading the way, I believe that the road to success will become easier. You must remind yourself every day that you have the ability to win. Never stop believing in yourself!

Skipper Back Home and Helping Colonials

By Richard Dalrymple
Eastern Eight Staff Writer

Photo by Henry Greenfield
SKIP SHOOTS—Wilbert Skipper, who transferred to GW this year from a junior college in Nebraska after playing his high school ball locally at Anacostia, has been a bright light for the Colonials this season with his shooting from the backcourt. Here he shoots against Georgetown earlier in the season. His story appears to the left.

(Continued on page 61)

★★★★★★★★★★★★★★★★★★★★★★★★★★

NOW PLAYING

TONIGHT
8 P.M.

GW BASKETBALL
At The Smith Center
VS
ST. BONAVENTURE

Earl Belcher, St. Bonaventure VS. Wilbert Skipper, GW

FOR INFORMATION: 676-DUNK

With McDonald's®
half-time shoot-out now worth $800

Big Mac® Sandwich Coupons Given Away To
First 1000 Fans

Skipper, Brey Lead GW In Rally Past Pitt, 79-74

By Donald Huff
Washington Post Staff Writer

George Washington may have grown up last night.

The youthful Colonials refused to be intimidated by big, bad Pittsburgh and rallied from a 12-point second-half deficit to steal a 79-74 decision in an Eastern Eight contest before 1,500 at the Smith Center.

The Colonials, now 2-0 in the conference and 7-4 overall, trailed, 47-35, with 17:33 left in the game before putting together probably their best second-half effort.

Sensational outside shooting by GW guards Wilbert Skipper (24 points) and Mike Brey (nine) got the Colonials back into the game. Brey, who rarely shoots (12 shots in four games), was left alone all night and the point guard finally decided to try a few. He burned Pitt's sagging zone for four straight 18-footers from the

first half because the shots weren't falling," said Brown, who finished with 21 points and 10 rebounds. "But they were good shots and they finally started falling."

Pitt Coach Roy Chipman wasn't as impressed with Brown's performance, blaming his team's defense.

"That was the worst defense we've played in two years," Chipman said. "We came out and jumped on them, going up by 12, then stopped playing basketball. There's absolutely no excuse for us giving up like that."

A steal and breakaway by Skipper gave the Colonials their biggest lead, 69-62, with 3:28 to play. But the hosts kept the game interesting by missing nine free throws, three of them on the front end of one and ones in the final five minutes.

"I had to be pleased," said GW Coach Gerry Gimelstob. "We didn't

Skipper on Mark Off the Bench For Colonials

By Kevin Tatum
Special to The Washington Star

When it was all over, George Washington University had beaten George Mason's Patriots by only 11 points, 80-69, last night at the Smith Center. But it didn't seem like it.

George Washington thoroughly dominated this one.

Even though the Patriots outrebounded GW, 34-29, and had four fewer turnovers (29-32), the Colonials were able to win with ease in a game both head coaches had expected to be a close.

"I thought we would win it," said Joe Harrington, head coach at George Mason. "We didn't really play that well but the difference was free throws."

(GW shot 70 percent from the line, George Mason 51 percent.)

"We played a sloppy game," said Harrington's counterpart, Bob Tallent of GW. "But we played well enough to win and that's what counts. I can't say that I expected to win like we did and maybe we wouldn't have if it hadn't been for Wilbert Skipper."

Neither coach was wrong in his appraisal of the contest, but the biggest single factor of the game was the play of Skipper, GW's third guard who finished with a game and personal high of 34 points.

Skipper came off the bench at the 10:06 mark of the first half with his team down 10-8. His first basket of the game tied it at 10-10 and he proceeded to score 14 points in the first half, all but one of them coming on jumpers from the 22- to 25-feet range.

Skipper's 14 points were one shy of George Mason's first-half total of 15. The Colonials had a 15-point lead at intermission, 30-15.

GW's Skipper Is Honored

Wilbert Skipper of George Washington University has been named to the Eastern Eight's All-Rookie team for the 1980-81 season.

Skipper, a 6-foot-3 junior guard out of Anacostia High School, averaged 14 points, mostly as the Colonials' third guard behind Curtis Jeffries and Randy Davis.

Norman Clarke of St. Bonaventure, Quentin Freeman of West Virginia, Edwin Green of Massachusetts and Clarence Tillman of Rutgers round out the all-rookie team.

DRIVING FOR THE LAYUP is senior Wilbert Skipper in Wednesday night's 63-62 upset of second place Rutgers. Skipper scored a season high 27 points in the win.

Skipper's 27 leads GW past Rutgers

by Mary-Ann Grams
Sport Editor

One point doesn't always make a difference in a sports event, but last night it did, as the the Colonials edged Rutgers 63-62 at the Smith Center in a crucial game that put GW (13-12, 7-6 conference) one game closer to a home court advantage in the Eastern Eight Tournament starting next Tuesday.

Wilbert Skipper, GW's senior guard, scored a GW season high 27 points and pulled down four rebounds to lead the Colonials. Freshman center Mike Brown also chipped in 17 points and grabbed 10 rebounds.

In the final seven seconds of the game, senior guard Mike Brey was fouled with the score 61-60 and he converted both free throws to bring the GW lead to three points. With a second left, Rutgers' Chris Remley hit a 10 foot jumper for two points, but it just wasn't enough as the Colonials triumphed over the Scarlet Knights 63-62 before a standing crowd in the Smith Center.

"The kind of effort that the guys gave tonight is what the whole game of college basketball is all about," commented head coach Gerry Gimelstob. "They (the players) have struggled and struggled all year and now they know that they have the chance to do anything that's possible. We'll probably get the home court advantage and that will be a great achievement for our team."

GW pulled ahead to an early lead in the first half with help from a strong pressure defense. Midway through the half the Colonials were up by seven at 21-14. The Scarlet Knights, however, from that point went on to score eight unanswered points to move ahead by one at 23-22. The lead then exchanged hands five times before the Colonials slowly moved to a 34-32 lead at the end of the first 20 minutes.

Rutgers slowly tied and regained the lead three times within the first five minutes of the second half play. The Colonials then went for six unanswered points in the next five minutes of play to hold a 48-42 lead. But a tap in by Rutgers' Chris Nieberlein and two layups by Kevin Black and Darius Griffin put the Scarlet Knights back in the game at 48-48. The Knights tied the score twice after, but were never able to regain the lead in the final 10 minutes.

Sophomore Dave Hobel chipped in eight points while sophomore forward Steve Perry added six and pulled down four rebounds. Senior Penny Elliott had seven rebounds in the contest.

Overall GW completed 51 percent of its shots from the floor while the Colonials averaged 76 percent completed from the free throw line.

The win put the Colonials in a tie for third place in the Eastern Eight with Pittsburgh, who lost last night 82-77 to first place West Virginia. If the Colonials can defeat Pitt on Saturday night in the Pittsburgh Civic Center, GW will be assured third place and a first round tournament game at home at the Smith Center.

Chapter 6

Co-workers

Have you ever worked in an environment where the boss or other employees suggested that *you* were the bad apple or the biggest problem in the workplace? I can personally relate to this issue. You may be able to identify with some of the negativity I experienced. In the late eighties, I worked in a hospital where many of my co-workers did not support my goals and dreams.

The more I talked about my future goals to establish a foundation to give back to my community, —even while giving my all to the company where I was employed—the more my co-workers began to separate themselves from me. Many people surprised me by actually telling me that I was fooling myself or that my current job was the best thing for me.

Sometimes co-workers do not want to see you advance above them. Because of my outside goals, I was seen as someone who thought I was better than they were; yet because of my belief in God, in myself, my focus, and my determination, I was able to stay positive.

Many people who work for someone else tend to become complacent. It is truly unfortunate how peer-pressure in the workforce can deter you from achieving success and reaching your goals. Some co-workers are very comfortable with knowing that they have a paycheck coming every payday; therefore, they do not want to jeopardize their comfort level by supporting you or taking risks for themselves. If you are a good employee and are extremely motivated about achieving goals inside and outside your workplace, you must trust in God, trust in yourself, and use the negative energy of your co-workers in a positive way. Some co-workers' negativity is simply envy of your abilities and determination to succeed.

My father once said, "When you step out in front, you should be prepared to become unpopular with most of your coworkers." However, stepping out in front should not be about losing a popularity contest; instead, it is about your desire to pursue your goals and dreams. Also, I know you have heard people say that there are leaders and then there are followers, and that it takes more guts to lead than to follow. Remember that those co-workers who envy you and do not believe you can achieve success beyond your current employment are potentially negative followers and dream stealers.

There is nothing wrong with working for someone else and feeling good about your current job, but I believe there is definitely something wrong with not wanting your co-workers to succeed or achieve their outside goals.

How many times have we heard co-workers say the following?

- "You'll end up right back here begging for your old job."
- "You must think you are better than everyone else or too good for this job."

- "Good luck trying to achieve your goal," (said with sarcasm)

On the other hand, has *this* occurred?

- Management or supervisors cast you negative looks because you mentioned your outside goals.
- Co-workers wished for your departure so that the work environment could be "normal."
- You thought twice about pursuing your goals in life because of the negativity in the work environment.
- Co-workers distanced themselves from you because they did not want other co-workers to think that they were supporting your efforts to succeed.
- Co-workers supported your efforts to succeed only halfway.
- You felt deep inside that many of your co-workers were just waiting for you to fail so that

they could say aloud, "I knew you wouldn't make it."

Co-workers can kill your dreams individually and collectively. One thing that we must remember is that your dreams and goals in life should always be more important to you than someone else's opinions—and your level of desire to achieve should always be high, no matter how hostile or negative the working environment might be. Staying focused and committed to your goals is by far one of the most important ingredients to your success.

There are co-workers who do support your success and positivity. For example, in 1998, while working in the produce department at Giant Foods in Landover, Maryland, my co-worker and I were having a conversation about life. He had a bad experience while on vacation with his family and was very upset. I was able see the silver lining in the situation; I told him that he could have been worse. After our conversation ended, he felt better, then smiled and said, "No matter how bad something might be in life, you always find something positive to say about it." I realize that nothing in life is a guarantee, but it does not hurt to make someone else smile by being truly positive. These are some of my co-workers who were supportive. For example, at Giant Foods, Cornell Smith, Craig Shelton, Bernie Fields, Tivie Booker, Nat Lewis, Jerome Phenious, and Barry Tolliver who truly believed in me. I really enjoyed talking with them about life outside of our workplace. They embraced the notion of future *success*.

As long as you are honest with God and true to yourself, you can achieve your goals outside of a work environment where many co-workers envy your drive to succeed. If you are dedicated to working hard, the only thing that can stop you is you. Do not be afraid of the *success* that God has prepared for you. It is *truly* a *blessing* because God does not make mistakes.

Chapter 7

Beware of the Dream Stealers

A dream stealer is anyone who purposely sets out to block, cripple, or destroy your dreams. No person is exempt from potentially becoming a dream stealer. Dream stealers can come in the form of family, friends, co-workers, church members, business associates, and strangers.

How many times in your life have you expressed your dreams or goals to someone, only to have them express doubt and disbelief about them in return? You must understand and accept that potential dream stealers can be discouraging. However, when you truly believe that you can succeed at something, there should never be any doubt about your ability to achieve it.

When you detect negative energy from someone, your positive will and way of thinking should immediately reflect moving forward. I know that this sounds very easy to do, but you may encounter people all along your path who, due to their internal misery and unhappiness, cannot envision your success. Sometimes, a person's ignorance can cause a negative outlook on your life. As you travel the long road to success, you must be able to weather the storms that you will likely face.

Once you begin to understand how a dream stealer thinks, you will be able to converse with them and use these negative thoughts in a positive way. Dream stealers create stress that can cripple your drive, determination, and readiness for future success. I have personally talked with many dream stealers and, after a few minutes of conversation, I knew that they were not going to be in my support group.

I personally believe that when you become very comfortable with yourself and your dreams, you should be able to use the negative energy of others as a motivating force for your success. Being able to weather any storm with God's divine power means that you cannot and dream stealers will not be able to stop you. When a dream stealer goes through the motions of placing doubt upon your goals and dreams, you must stay focused; continue to be determined to pursue your future success.

When you are secure with God's blessings and yourself, dream stealers do not intimidate you. Think positively, be positive, and live positively despite the negative energy from others.

Understand that your dreams are worth pursuing. They are within your reach. You must say to yourself every day that you have a God-given ability to achieve higher heights, despite what someone else believes. You have to paint a picture of success on all levels in your life before you will be able to achieve your future prosperity. Once this level of belief is within your thought processes, you can easily block out the thoughts of the dream stealers.

A dream stealer is not ignorant to the possibility of your future success; he or she simply feels better when you fail. Dream stealers have the ability to make you feel like your hard work is a waste of time and effort.

How to recognize a dream stealer:

- Someone who constantly says "You wouldn't be good at that
- Someone who is always negative
- Someone who try to deter you from reaching your highest potential

Keeping a positive attitude about living everyday is one way of dealing with dream stealers. When a dream stealer appears before you, the "thinking positive" light switch must immediately click on. When you fight back with negative energy, your positive way of thinking and feeling begins to weaken. The weaker you become in life, the better chance the dream stealer has to claim victory. Most dream stealers love to say, "I told you so," and, "I knew you couldn't do it."

Let go of things you cannot change or control because your positive energy will help defy the naysayers and the dream stealers. You must be able to stand alone in your beliefs. Say no to those who do not believe in you and your journey; say yes to God's plans for you, which cannot be stopped by any man or woman on this earth. You must never subject yourself to a dream stealer's way of thinking. Never doubt your ability to achieve the best that God has in store for you. Jealous dream stealers are people that life has passed them by. They will give up any opportunity to live their dreams and they can't stand to see you succeed where they fail.

When I was thirteen years old and trying out for the Douglas Junior High basketball team, there were many people who told me that I should give up on playing basketball and just become part of a street group. They believed that there was no way out of the neighborhood in which we lived. Some thought that since many of the people around me had no inclination toward becoming successful, then I should be the same way. I had bigger dreams for myself.

I immediately told myself that I was going to work extra hard on my basketball skills so that I could prove those people wrong. I wanted to let them know and show them that no matter where you grow up and how bad it may seem, there is always hope for everyone. If I can do it—you can, too!

I envisioned my future success in my mind, before it became a reality. During this time, there continued to be many dream stealers in my neighborhood who truly believed in their own goals and dreams for me—which were for me to fail! They tried to influence me to do negative things that I knew was wrong. I never looked for validation from others. God gave me the internal and external strength that I needed to prevail against the naysayers and the dream stealers.

Once you are determined to achieve something good, you should not allow someone to destroy or hamper your future success. To cultivate a tough skin while dealing with dream stealers is very important. I have found that sometimes, someone who is playing the role of a dream stealer can destroy a very personal and loving relationship. When this happens, you must turn on the "I can make it" vision and turn off the negative energy associated with the dream stealer.

Why should you allow someone to steal your dreams after you have put in countless hours of hard work toward your future success? When I look back on my teenage life, I cannot forget about the many dream stealers who consistently told me that my dreams of becoming a great basketball player were nothing more than a lie to myself.

Unfortunately, sometimes the people who you truly trust and believe in do not feel the same way about you. To pray for them is a good thing, but to agree with their actions is not a good formula for achieving your future success. Because dream stealers work very hard at keeping you down mentally, you must be able to combat their efforts by continuing to believe that you can achieve your goals and dreams. You must always believe that you are more than worthy of what God has outlined for you. Knowing how and when to shield yourself from the power of a dream stealer is very important to your continuing motivation and focus toward your future success.

You should never complicate your journey to success by keeping a dream stealer in your corner. You must be able to take the high road to success. That road is simply continuing to believe in God and to strengthen your motivation, focus, determination, and belief in yourself. When you allow someone to invalidate you based on his or her beliefs, sometimes you fall short of what you believe.

There is nothing wrong with someone believing in you, but you must always be a believer in yourself. Another good recipe for success is unlimited doses of God, many helpings of the willpower to endure, and having the determination and focus volume set to a high level.

Being able to turn off the negative energy from a dream stealer who can drain your positive way of thinking is very important.
This method consists of the following:

- Do not allow a dream stealer to cripple your drive and motivation to win every day.
- Continue to believe in your ability to succeed.
- Remain focused and allow your positive way of thinking to shine.
- Know that God wants you to be the best that you can be at all times, which should allow you to reach back and help others.

Bear in mind dream stealers are in fact negative people and people that really don't have any goals or know what to do with their life. Never try to confront a dream stealer because they are not aware that you are in a state of awareness beyond theirs. Simply move on while encouraging them to follow their dreams because they are the people that need it the most.

For Example:

- Writing his or her words down and tearing them up to remove them from your mind.
- Remember that ignorance or a person repeated setbacks can be what gives him or her the voice of doubt.
- Take the one positive thing you gleaned from the bad conversation, write it down, and tape it to a mirror.

- Evaluate whether you should continue being friends with this person

- If this is a family member, draw a boundary, saying, "I love you, but we are going to have to agree to disagree about my choice and its best we not discuss it further."

- Imagine flicking on your "positive light" as you walk away from that person.

Conclusion

I hope that the tools and suggestions provided here will help in your pursuit of your goals and dreams. Always remember that no man or woman on this earth can take God's plan away from you. Continue to stay focused, believe in yourself, and use your God-given talent to achieve your goals and help others. I will see you in the success line!

Remember, "Yes, You Can." With God in your life, all things are more than possible!

Special thanks for their support:

Jon Jones has been a true friend and a sincere believer in my ability to succeed for over twenty years. His dedication to God and spiritual presence in my life has been a true blessing to me.

Bob Talent, GWU head basketball coach 1980–81, was supportive of my individual basketball talents, and he welcomed me to the GW family with open arms. He was a great coach.

The late Len Baltimore, GWU Assistant Basketball Coach 1980–81, was relentless in his recruiting of me. With his help, I accepted a basketball scholarship to play at GWU and replaced Brian Magid, a great outside shooter.

Mike Patrick (ESPN sports analyst) often encouraged me when he was the basketball voice of the George Washington University Colonials.

Merlin Friend, who was the GWU Assistant Basketball Coach during my 1981–82 seasons, was a big influence and positive supporter of my basketball career.

Mr. Richard Mosby (Douglas Jr. High basketball coach) prepared me for many of the pitfalls in life while playing basketball at Douglas Junior High School.

Chuck Taylor and Rock Greene (United States Youth Game) gave me the opportunity to better my game and basketball talents while representing the DC Team in Forth Worth, Texas.

The late Calvin Stith (basketball coach) helped me to grow as a basketball player while at Anacostia High School. His mental toughness prepared me for college basketball and life after.

Allen Chin was very instrumental in keeping me focused on my goals after basketball.

Greg Hunter, CEO of Capacity Funding, provided professional advice and invaluable support.

Eugene Hellams Jr., CEO of Hellams Fitness, gave genuine support and encouragement regarding my physical fitness.

Fred Shepard Jr. (a.k.a. One-Shot Fred), contributed excellent photography work, dedication, and support.

Malick Wade, president of Metro Area Consulting, LLC, offered both support and friendship over the years.

Buddy Love Productions provided excellent advice, support, and production expertise.

Wanda Childs, motivational speaker and author of *Pushed into My Purpose,* extended her professional and first-hand knowledge about the task of becoming a self-published author. Her master teachings and God-given talents have been a blessing to me.

Kevin T. Robertson, professional keynote speaker, business trainer, author, and host of a TV and Internet show, provided guidance, wisdom, and focused strategies regarding my pursuit of becoming an author and motivational speaker. He has been a great supporter of my goals and dreams.

Nasir Shahid was very supportive regarding my book writing campaign.

Greg Weston gave me an opportunity to display my speaking skills and learn from a great communicator.

Douglas Donaldson helped me develop and improve my speaking skills. His passion for assisting others is a great asset.

Additional thanks goes to the following:

Mike Lonergan, Current GWU Head Basketball Coach

Karl Hobbs, former George Washington University head basketball coach

GWU Athletic Department

Curtis Bunn, bestselling author, *Essence Magazine*

Adrian Branch, motivational speaker, ESPN sports

James Brown, NFL sports anchor, author

My sisters, Censeria Patton and Kimyanna Farmearl

Mr. and Mrs. Sewards, Sewards Unisex Hair Salon

First Rate Cleaning Services (CEO, Richard Footes)

Pennington Greene, founder of the DC basketball blog

Steve Ardekani, Carpet Queen & Floors (Owner)

Jerome Tucker, host of Third Eye Open, blog talk radio

Red Groover, SCC Nebraska

Paul Shuttlesworth, SCC Nebraska, basketball coach and English professor

Mr. and Mrs. Klugie and family

Steve Hunter, SCC Basketball 1978–80

Coach Tillery, Douglass Junior HS recreation coach

Nana Prince Baduh, author of the Obama inaugural poems

Ernest Cashwell and the late Mr. Edward Harris, Seat Pleasant Barber Shop

Lawrence Yates, Pee Wee, former coach of Tennis Haven basketball team

The late Coach Brown, Anacostia High School

Silky Smooth Dance Studio

Al Hall, George Washington Security Department

Linda Crop, former Chair DC City Council

Steve Powell, former Howard University football coach

Coach Muel, Anacostia High School

Don Briscoe

Derrick Jackson, Shooter Sports

Clarence G. Singleton, Native Son Video & Designs

Steve Williams (Hawk) Anacostia Alumnus

Cornell Adams, Anacostia Alumnus

Anthony Bethea, Anacostia Alumnus

Listed below are some of the Douglass Junior High School Basketball fraternity members:

Carroll High School

Eddie Jordan, Former Washington Wizards and Philadelphia 76ers Head Basketball Coach

Ballou High School

Doren Dent, Stan Simpson, Kool Parker, Mike Wise, Steve Macullor, Vincent Askew, Butch Folkes, Skip Folkes, Super Chick (great ball handler and floor general), Mo Wilson, Keith Tanner, Sylvester Askew, Kenny Craig Keith Craig, Curtis Bunn, Charles Chisley, Bo Thompson, Mike Ryan, and Darryl Sheffy

Anacostia High School

Charles "Chuck" Jackson, Ronald Wilson, William Marlbury, James "Chip" Coach, John Mayo, Eugene "Fatty" Thompson, Sheldon Edwards, Walter Wright, Frank Bluford, and Jeff Bluford

Other High Schools

Allen Tate, Chamberlin High School

The late Butch Hill, St. Albans

Gary Jordan, James Rochea, McKinley Tech High School

Tyrone Edwards, Chamberlin High School

Darryl Edwards, Western High School and Bernard Edwards-Coolidge, High School

11294909R00054

Made in the USA
San Bernardino, CA
13 May 2014